SWISS
NARROW GAUGE
featuring steam in the Alps

John Organ
Series editor Vic Mitchell

MP Middleton Press

Cover pictures:
Front: Furka-Oberalp 2-6-0RT no.3 heads a special train from Disentis to Brig at Oberalppasshöhe on 24th September 1967. It is many years since a steam hauled train traversed this eastern section of the FO route. (J.Wiseman).
Rear: A close up view of Rhätische Bahn 2-8-0 no.107 as it waits at Filisur, whilst hauling a charter train from Preda to Chur on 27th May 1967. (D.Trevor Rowe).

Published March 2003

ISBN 1 901706 94 X

© Middleton Press, 2003

Design   Deborah Esher
            David Pede
Typesetting Barbara Mitchell

Published by
            Middleton Press
            Easebourne Lane
            Midhurst, West Sussex
            GU29 9AZ
Tel: 01730 813169
Fax: 01730 812601
Email: enquiries@middletonpress.fsnet.co.uk

Printed & bound by Biddles Ltd,
            Guildford and Kings Lynn

CONTENTS

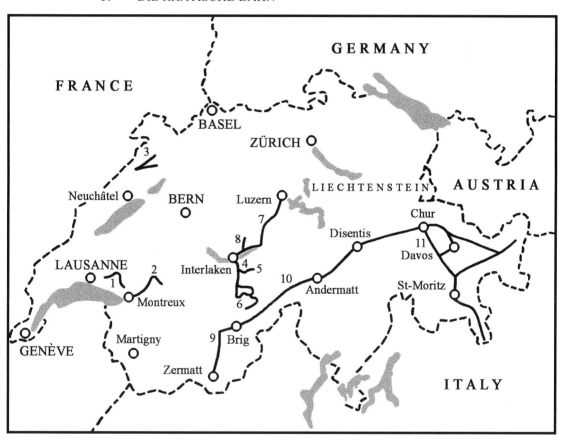

INTRODUCTION

The mountain chain known collectively as The Alps runs from South East France, across the entire length of Southern Switzerland and finally much of Southern Austria. Also embraced is the northern area of Italy and part of Slovenia, much of which was formerly under Austrian control prior to the boundary changes following World War I.

The Alpine regions of Switzerland and Austria are interlaced with an amazing network of Narrow Gauge Railways. These serve as feeders to the main line systems and are in some cases very extensive systems in their own right. The majority of the Swiss metre gauge lines are privately owned, although receiving much financial assistance from the Cantons through which they operate. Only one Swiss narrow gauge line is part of the state owned Swiss Federal Railways / *Schweizerische Bundesbahnen* (SBB) system, which was formed in 1902. Although metre gauge was adopted for the conventional routes, 80cm was used for the majority of the purely rack and pinion mountain lines.

Although Switzerland adopted electrification for the majority of its railway network during the early years of the 20th century, many steam locomotives were retained both on the SBB standard gauge system and many of the privately owned narrow gauge lines. Initially retained for emergency use such as snow clearing duties, the attractions of steam hauled trains on some of the more scenic routes was quickly recognised and these have become a regular feature during the summer months. Additionally, Switzerland can boast three major tourist lines that feature steam operations as an everyday service. One of these, that currently is in the course of rebuilding a closed section of the original route, has recently imported four of the lines original locomotives from Vietnam. These were exported to the Far East following electrification of the line 60 years ago.

Almost without exception, all steam locomotives built in Switzerland were the products of one concern. This is the *Schweizerische Lokomotiv und Maschinenfabrik,* Winterthur (SLM), a manufacturer that will be frequently mentioned in this publication.

This book will attempt to cover the major narrow gauge steam and electric operations in the alpine regions of Switzerland. Using archive views and current scenes on some of the most scenic railways in Europe, the flavour of the contrasting systems of this small country will be most apparent.

ACKNOWLEDGEMENTS

In compiling this book, I have been very fortunate in having received much valuable assistance from a large number of fellow enthusiasts. My thanks are due to Mr. N.Britton, Mr. R.Elkin, Monsieur B.Gueret (BVA), Mr. A.Heywood, Mr. J.Marsh, Photoglobe-CH, Mr. D.Trevor Rowe, Mr. D.Smith, Mr. C.Stone, Mr. K.Taylorson, Mr. R. de Wardt, Mr. J.K.Williams and Mr. J.Wiseman. I must also add a special word of thanks to my wife Brenda, who has once again tolerated my deep involvement in the subject during the period of research and preparation.

1. SWISS NARROW GAUGE STEAM LOCOMOTIVES

Despite the electrification of the majority of the Swiss railway network at an early stage in its development, a large number of steam locomotives were supplied by SLM for the many narrow gauge lines. These ranged from conventional machines for use on the adhesion lines, powerful rack and adhesion locomotives for the routes including rack sections and finally the purely rack and pinion designs for the mountain lines.

Many of the adhesion lines were situated away from the mountainous regions and consequently locomotives of modest power output were sufficient for their motive power requirements. The majority of these were simple 0-6-0Ts (G 3/3), not unlike the many similar locomotives supplied by the French manufacturers for use in that country. A typical example of these small metre gauge locomotives has been preserved at the *CFT Blonay-Chamby.* Constructed in 1901 for use on the Brünig section of the SBB, it was transferred to the *Bières-Apples-Morges* (BAM) in the west of Switzerland in 1921.

With the construction of lines requiring more powerful locomotives to cope with steep gradients, an enlarged 2-6-0T (G 3/4) version of this standard design was introduced in 1889. These handsome locomotives were one of the most successful narrow gauge designs to emerge from the SLM works at Winterthur. The two railways that were synonymous with this version were the *Rhätische Bahn* (RhB) and the SBB *Brünig* line. As will be recorded in the relevant chapters, three of the RhB locomotives and one of the later SBB variants have survived in working order in Switzerland. In addition, other examples were sold to Greece where at least three locomotives are reputedly in store.

Although designed by a Swiss engineer, Anatole Mallet, the articulated locomotives that bore his name were only used by one Swiss railway. The RhB Mallets supplied between 1891 and 1902 as 0-4-4-0Ts, 0-4-4-2Ts and 2-4-4-0Ts were intended to handle the heavy trains on that large and steeply graded system. Surprisingly they didn't prove to be as successful in their native land as, for example, the many similar locomotives employed on the French metre gauge lines. Consequently, no examples of these interesting machines have survived either in Switzerland or any of the countries to which they were sold after their withdrawal from service on the RhB.

Derived from a standard gauge design, the most successful metre gauge adhesion locomotives were the 2-8-0 (G 4/5) tender locomotives supplied to the RhB between 1904 and 1915. As will be noted in chapter 5, two of these powerful workhorses have been retained by the RhB and are a familiar sight hauling vintage rolling stock on special charter trains throughout the year. At least two more have survived as static exhibits in Thailand, 18 of the class having been exported there following completion of the electrification of the RhB. The earliest examples were built as compounds, although sadly none of those have survived.

The locomotives supplied for use on the rack and adhesion lines were of three basic designs. These comprised of 0-4-2RT (HG 2/3), 0-6-0RT (HG 3/3), derived from an earlier 0-4-0RT version, and 2-6-0RT (HG 3/4) designs, examples of all three types are still in service. The 0-4-2RTs were supplied to the Abt system *Visp-Zermatt Bahn* (VZ) between 1891 and 1906. Although relatively small locomotives, these superheated four cylinder compound machines proved capable of hauling trains up the steep gradients on the 36km line between Visp and Zermatt. Two have survived, one of which still works on its native route whilst the other has been preserved on the rebuilt mountain section of the neighbouring *Furka-Oberalp-Bahn.*

The 0-6-0RTs introduced in 1905 were fitted with the Riggenbach system of rack equipment, for use on the Brünig line of the SBB. Unlike the smaller VZ design, these four cylinder compound locomotives were not superheated. However, they were very powerful and proved equally at home hauling trains up the 1 in 9 rack sections of the Brünig Pass or along the relatively flat conventional sections of the route. Three of these machines have been preserved in their native land whilst at least two are believed to be in store in Greece.

The most successful rack and adhesion design were the 2-6-0RTs supplied in 1913 and 1914 for use on the *Brig-Furka-Disentis* (BFD) line. These superheated four cylinder compound locomotives were equipped with Abt system rack equipment and were more than equal to the task of hauling heavy trains over the 1 in 9 inclines of the Furka and Oberalp passes. With their impressive performance matched by an equally impressive appearance, these were the definitive Swiss narrow gauge locomotives. As will be related in the relevant chapter, following the electrification of the Furka line all but two of these locomotives were sold to the Far East. One of the Swiss survivors is now to be found working on the Blonay-Chamby line whilst the other has remained on its home territory. During the last decade four of the emigrant locomotives have been repatriated whilst there are possibly another four decaying in a Vietnam jungle clearing!

The locomotives supplied for use on the purely rack and pinion mountain railways were basically of one type. These were 0-4-2RTs (H 2/3) with their boilers and cabs inclined at a steep angle to compensate for the steep gradients on which they operated. However, the original rack and pinion locomotives supplied in 1871 were standard gauge machines with a vertical boiler. One of these improbable looking creations was the first locomotive to be built by SLM in 1873 and has consequently been preserved. It was returned to working order in 1996 for use on the *Rigi Bahnen* in conjunction with the 125th anniversary celebrations of that line, the oldest of the Swiss mountain railways.

The 0-4-2RTs, which first appeared in 1891, are synonymous with the 80cm *Brienz Rothorn Bahn* (BRB) where three of the original locomotives are still in service, plus two more acquired from other lines. Known affectionately as "kneeling cow" locomotives, the drive was provided by two double toothed pinions fixed to each driving axle. The running wheels on these axles revolved freely whilst the cylinders were mounted alongside the boiler. The motion was transmitted to the drive cranks via vertically mounted rocking levers at the front of the locomotive. These levers connected the upper and lower connecting rods, reducing the crank throw in order to provide the necessary gear reductions. Locomotives of a similar design work on the Snowdon Mountain Railway, although their boilers are inclined at a far less acute angle than their Swiss counterparts.

An updated superheated version of the same design was introduced in 1933, two examples being supplied to the BRB. In place of the rocking levers of the earlier design, the pistons were connected to a sophisticated system of gearing mounted below the smokebox. With a lower drive ratio available, these proved to be far more powerful locomotives in service and are still in regular use today.

In 1988 SLM produced a new design of oil fired 0-4-2RT, the first of which was delivered to the BRB in 1992. Designed for one-man operation these machines incorporate many modern technical features in their design, allowing a rapid availability with the ability to retain boiler heat overnight due to improved thermal insulation. Additionally, an external electrical pre-heater can heat the water of a cold boiler very quickly without constant supervision.

In addition to the three locomotives supplied to the BRB, another works on the MTGN whilst a number of metre gauge examples have been supplied to Austria. These extremely powerful and economic locomotives bear more than a passing resemblance to the standard gauge 0-4-2RTs supplied to the Rigi line in 1925.

1.1.   RhB 2-6-0T no.1 "Rhätia" is seen displayed at Chamby on 15th September 1974. This was the first locomotive supplied to the* Landquart-Davos-Bahn, *forerunner of the RhB, in 1889 and was returned to its original home in 1989, following many years as part of the Blonay-Chamby collection. Prior to 1967, this historic locomotive had been on display in the Swiss Transport Museum at Luzern. (J.K.Williams)

1.2.   A later version of the same design, SBB no.208 was built in 1913. This handsome locomotive was photographed at Brienz in September 1988 whilst hauling a train from Meiringen to Interlaken on the metre gauge Brünig section of the state system. (J.F.Organ)

1.3.   One of the former RhB 2-4-4-0T Mallets was still in service on a Spanish industrial line in April 1961. Sadly none of these Swiss locomotives have survived, although similar Swiss built machines are still at work in France. (D.Trevor Rowe)

1.4.   RhB 2-8-0 no.107 stands on the turntable at Preda, after hauling a charter train from Chur on 27ᵗʰ May 1967. Note the briquettes stacked on top of the tender. (D. Trevor Rowe)

1.5.   This is one of the original 2-8-0 compound locomotives supplied to the RhB. Retaining its former number 104, it was still at work in Spain on the La Robla Railway on 14ᵗʰ April 1961. (D. Trevor Rowe)

1.6.   SBB 0-6-0RT no.1067 was photographed at Interlaken in 1963. This 4 cylinder compound rack and adhesion locomotive was built in 1910 for use on the Brünig line between Meiringen and Giswil, where it is still in use hauling charter trains. (F.Ward/J.K.Williams coll.)

1.7.   Visp-Zermatt- Bahn 0-4-2RT no.7 stands at Stalden on 29th May 1967, whilst working a special train from Brig to Zermatt. Although smaller than the SBB 0-6-0RTs these locomotives, introduced in 1891, had the advantage of superheating and proved to be very capable performers. (D.Trevor Rowe)

1.8. *The definitive rack and adhesion design were the* **Furka-Oberalp-Bahn 2-6-0RTs** *which date from 1913. One of these powerful handsome locomotives was photographed at Blonay on 2nd September 1990, restored to its original condition as* **Brig-Furka-Disentis (BFD) no.3.** *(J.F. Organ)*

1.9. *The predecessors of the familiar "kneeling cow" 0-4-2RT locomotives were the vertical boiler 0-4-0RTs supplied to the standard gauge* **Vitznau-Rigi Bahn.** *One of these improbable looking creations, no.7, was the first locomotive to be constructed by SLM in 1873. It was restored to working order in 1996 and is seen at Rigi-Kulm in September of that year. (C.R.Stone)*

1.10. This is one of the first 0-4-2RT rack and pinion locomotives supplied to the **Brienz-Rothorn-Bahn** in 1891. No 2, is seen at Brienz in July 1981, before propelling a train to the summit. The steeply inclined boiler and cab is very noticeable in this view, their description as "kneeling cows" being very apt. (J.Marsh)

1.11. A century later, SLM were once again building 0-4-2RT locomotives, albeit of a far more advanced design. Oil fired MTGN no.1, delivered in 1992, at Rochers De Naye where it was photographed on 12ᵗʰ August 1997. (D.Trevor Rowe)

2. MONTREUX AND THE JURA REGION

Montreux, situated on the northern shore of Lake Geneva (*Lac Léman*), is well known as a resort of the rich and famous. For railway enthusiasts it is recognised as one of the few locations in Europe where lines of three gauges converge in one station. The main part of Montreux station is occupied by the standard gauge tracks of the SBB Rhône Valley route. Across the island platform of the eastbound SBB tracks is the terminus of the metre gauge *Montreux-Oberland-Bernois* (MOB), which links Montreux with Zweisimmen by a delightfully scenic 88 km route constructed between 1901 and 1905. Finally on the other side of the station forecourt is the 80 cm rack and pinion line that climbs to the Rochers-de-Naye, requiring 10 km to reach its 1973m upper terminus. Apart from the occasional main line special, steam locomotives have long ceased to be a common sight at Montreux. However a short distance to the north of the lakeside town is to be found the most comprehensive collection of metre gauge motive power in Switzerland.

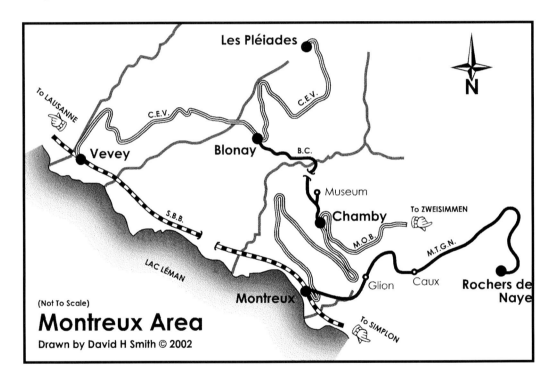

(Not To Scale)

Montreux Area

Drawn by David H Smith © 2002

Chemin de Fer Touristique Blonay-Chamby

A short distance from Montreux is the neighbouring resort of Vevey. From there a metre gauge rack and adhesion line runs to Les Pléiades, known as the *Chemins de fer Électriques Veveysans* (CEV). The two sections, completed in 1902 and 1911 respectively, join at Blonay. This is also the junction of a 3 km line linking the CEV to the MOB at Chamby, which was opened in 1902 in conjunction with the lower section of the CEV. Although originally separate enterprises, the CEV was amalgamated with the MOB in 1990.

The short connecting line saw little commercial traffic for many years and in 1966 was closed, although the track and electrical equipment was left in place. A railway enthusiast group based in Lausanne saw this "mothballed" line as an ideal base for a museum railway and active discussions were initiated with the CEV. The result was the formation of the *CFT Blonay-Chamby* in 1968. Whilst locomotives and rolling stock were gradually being purchased from around Europe, a large site adjacent to the track at Chaulin, a short distance below Chamby, was excavated for the erection of a large museum and workshop complex. Whilst the first exhibits were delivered to Chaulin in January 1967, it wasn't until 20th July 1968 that the first revenue earning train was operated by the infant organisation.

Although only 3 km in length, the steeply graded line which climbs 130m between Blonay and Chamby, is an exemplary example of Swiss narrow gauge practice combined in one short line. Leaving the junction at Blonay, the route crosses a minor road before ascending through meadowland behind the villas of Blonay. After a short distance it enters a woodland area where it crosses a curving 6 arch viaduct. The other major civil engineering feature of the line is the 45 metre long tunnel, which emerges at the intermediate halt of Cornaux. There then follows the final climb past Chaulin to the upper terminus at Chamby, alongside the MOB station. As electric traction is an important part of the collection, the route is electrified by an overhead system of 900 volts DC.

A total of twelve steam locomotives, plus a steam powered rotary snow plough, are joined by three electric locomotives and a large assortment of electric railcars and trams. Naturally a large collection of passenger and freight rolling stock is also an important part of the collection. The latter are representative of metre gauge railways throughout Switzerland plus some examples from France. Likewise the electric traction is wholly of Swiss origin, the largest example being a Ge 4/4 (BoBo) built in 1916 for the *Bernina Bahn* (later to be incorporated into the *Rhätische Bahn*). Originally a Ge 6/6 (CoCo) locomotive, it was rebuilt to its current form in 1929. However it is the superb collection of steam power for which the Blonay-Chamby is most renowned.

The collection includes examples from Switzerland, France, Germany, Spain and Italy. These range from a diminutive 0-4-0TR "Bi-Cabine" from Padane in Italy and a slightly larger 2-4-2TR "Bi-Cabine" from the *Tramways de Mulhouse* in France. Switzerland is represented by three 0-6-0Ts, from various lines in the western part of the country and one of the powerful 2-6-0RT rack and pinion fitted locomotives from the *Furka-Oberalp Bahn*. The latter has been restored in its original *Brig-Furka-Disentis* (BFD) livery. From France there is one of the splendid *Réseau Breton* 4-6-0Ts whilst Spain is represented by a 2-6-2T from the *Olat-Gerona* line. Finally, the largest locomotives are of German origin. These include a brace of Mallets, a 0-6-6-0T and a 0-4-4-0T plus a 0-10-0T. For many years, Chaulin was also the home of locomotive no.1 from the *Rhätische Bahn* (RhB), a 2-6-0T built in 1889. However this was returned to its original home in 1989 in order to participate in the centenary of the RhB where it has remained, being regularly used on special excursions. The museum at Chaulin is also the home of one of the impressive steam powered rotary snowploughs from the RhB, although the chance of it being used for its original purpose at its current home is very remote. A complete list of the steam locomotives in the collection is included at the end of this chapter.

In addition to hauling trains on the short Blonay-Chamby line, some of the larger locomotives are occasionally allowed to "stretch their legs" by hauling special excursions on the tracks of the MOB and the neighbouring *Chemin de fer Gruyères-Fribourg-Morat* (GFM). Normally these duties are allocated to the Breton 4-6-0T or one of the German locomotives.

As a wholly volunteer organisation, the Blonay-Chamby activities are restricted to Saturdays and Sundays between May and October. However, an intensive service is operated on those days with steam hauled trains alternating with those using electric traction. Chamby is easily reached by rail using the MOB between Montreux and Zweisimmen, whilst Blonay is likewise easily accessible via the CEV from Vevey. For those arriving by road, Blonay has ample parking facilities and is easily reached from Vevey or Montreux.

Steam Locomotives of the CFT Blonay-Chamby

Type	Constructor	Year Built	Origin
0-6-0T (G 3/3)	SLM	1890	Régional des Brenets
2-6-0T (G 3/4)	SLM	1889	Rhätische Bahn (To RhB 1989)
2-6-0RT (HG 3/4)	SLM	1914	Furka-Oberalp
0-4-0TR (G 2/2)	Krauss (Munich)	1900	Ferrovie Padane (Italy)
0-6-0T (G 3/3)	SACM	1890	Lausanne-Echallens-Bercher
0-6-0T (G 3/3)	SLM	1901	Bière-Apples-Morges
2-4-2TR (G 2/4)	SLM	1882	Tramways de Mulhouse (France)
2-6-2T (G 3/5)	MTM	1926	Olot-Gerona (Spain)
4-6-0T (G 3/5)	Fives-Lille	1909	Réseau Breton (France)
0-6-6-0T (G 2 x 3/3)	Hanomag	1925	Zell-Todtnau (Germany)
0-4-4-0T (G 2 x 2/2)	Karlsruhe	1918	Zell-Todtnau (Germany)
0-10-0T (G 5/5)	Esslingen	1927	Nagold-Altensteig (Germany)

Montreux-Rochers De Naye Railway

Across the forecourt of the station at Montreux is the now closed Hotel Terminus, of somewhat faded Victorian grandeur. Below the patio adjoining the main entrance of this hotel is the lower terminus of the 80cm Abt system rack and pinion line that ascends to the Rochers-De-Naye via Glion and Caux. Originally opened between Glion (which is the upper station of a water balance controlled funicular from Territet) and the summit in 1892 as a steam operated railway, it was connected to Montreux in 1902 when the lower section of the line was constructed. However, due to the close proximity of the residential suburbs of Montreux, the lower section was electrically operated from the outset using a 750 volts DC supply. The original section from Glion continued to be steam operated until July 1938 when it was converted to electric traction compatible with the lower section. At around the same period, the *Chemin de fer Montreux-Territet-Glion-Naye* (MTGN) as it had been renamed, was amalgamated with the MOB.

The SLM 0-4-2RT steam locomotives were sold, and the line seemed destined to remain wholly electrified for the remainder of its existence. Modern two-car units were supplied in 1983 and an intensive all year round service has continued to operate. Whilst the summer is busy with tourists wishing to explore the scenic delights of the Rochers De Naye (the views from the summit are superb) and the cuisine of the Hotel des Rochers, winter sees hoards of ski enthusiasts bound for the popular ski slopes.

With the tourist market in mind, steam returned to the MTGN in 1992 when one of the "new generation" 0-4-2RT oil fired rack and pinion locomotives produced by SLM was delivered. This modern machine makes light work of the 1 in 4½ gradients between Caux and the summit, pushing two heavily loaded vintage coaches retained from earlier days. As in the previous steam operated era, these trains are restricted to the upper section of the line - even Glion is now within the suburban conurbation of Montreux where the operation of a steam locomotive, albeit oil fired, would be considered environmentally unfriendly! However, the steam propelled journey along the upper reaches of the line to the 1973m summit station, set in the bowl of an extinct volcanic crater, is a splendid experience and operates regularly between Spring and Autumn.

Chemins de Fer du Jura

Situated on the French border north of Geneva, the Jura region of Switzerland is not part of the alpine area. However this delightful area of woodland and lush hillsides possesses an interesting network of metre gauge railways. They were the last system in the country to rely on steam haulage, electrification not being completed until 1953. Of more importance to this publication, the popularity of steam hauled "tourist" trains was realised by the management of the *CF du Jura* (CJ) during the last decade. Having scrapped its original motive power in 1953, they had to look elsewhere for replacements to operate these proposed trains.

With no suitable locomotives available for purchase in Switzerland, the CJ turned to Portugal and acquired two Mallets, a number of which were available, surplus to requirements. Both products of Henschel, a 0-4-4-0T no. E 164 and a 2-4-6-0T no. E 206, dating from 1905 and 1913 respectively, were purchased in 1992 and sent back to Germany for restoration.

The two locomotives are based at Pré-Petitjean, near Saignelégier and are used regularly throughout the summer months over the various routes of the CJ. These radiate from Saignelégier to destinations such as Glovelier, Tavannes and Le Chaux-de-Fonds. The latter location is of interest to enthusiasts as it includes a section of street running through the town, where the large Mallet locomotives dominate the scene somewhat.

Although these trains operate on a number of dates between July and September, prior seat reservations are recommended for potential travellers. The relevant address and telephone number is listed in the appendix of this publication.

2.1. *Three gauges at Montreux. In September 1990 a Re 4/4 11 locomotive of the SBB passes through the station, with an express bound for Brig, whilst a MOB metre gauge railcar waits in the bay platform. In the distance can be seen an 80cm gauge railcar of the MTGN. (J.F.Organ)*

2.2. *Former Réseau Breton 4-6-0T no. E 332 is in the headshunt at Chamby station, whilst acting as a three dimensional advertisement for the CFT Blonay-Chamby in September 1969. (J.Wiseman)*

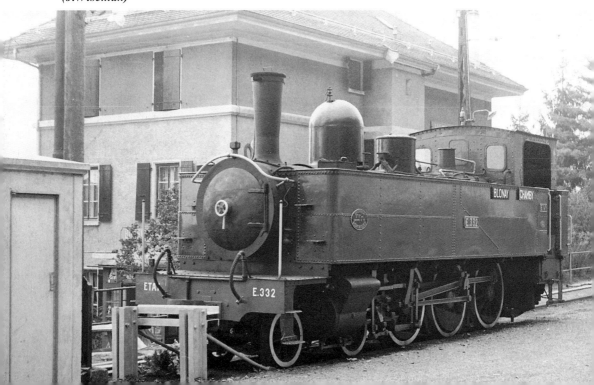

2.3.   *0-6-0T no.6, formerly of the SBB Brünig line and BAM, waits at the Chaulin depot of the Blonay-Chamby on 10th June 2001. This locomotive, dating from 1901, is a typical example of those supplied for use on the metre gauge lines in the west and north of Switzerland. The electric locomotive in the background was built in 1913 for an industrial railway at Schaffhausen. (D.Trevor Rowe)*

2.4.   *RhB Ge 4/4 no.181 was photographed at Chaulin on 2nd September 1990. Formerly no.81 of the Bernina Bahn and built in 1916 as a Ge 6/6, this is the largest electric locomotive in the Blonay-Chamby collection. (J.F.Organ)*

2.5.　　The three German locomotives of the Blonay-Chamby collection were displayed in the large depot at Chaulin in September 1990. The Esllingen 0-10-0T is in the foreground with the Hanomag 0-6-6-0T Mallet behind. On the left is the Karlsruhe 0-4-4-0T Mallet undergoing a major overhaul. (J.F.Organ)

2.6.　　Furka-Oberalp 2-6-0RT no.3 is at the coaling stage at Chaulin on 2nd September 1990. The main running line of the B-C is seen to the left of the photograph. (J.F.Organ)

2.7.   **No.3 drifts down the bank towards Blonay on the same occasion. The second coach is a former** Réseau Breton *vehicle incorporating a luggage compartment. (J.F.Organ)*

2.8. *The 0-4-4-0T Mallet nears the summit of the climb near Chamby on 6th September 1969. With only two coaches to haul, the powerful locomotive was not exactly overworked at this early stage of the Blonay-Chamby tourist operation. (J.Wiseman)*

2.9. *On the same date, no.105 arrives at Blonay with a train from Chamby. To the right of the road is the old formation of an electric tramway that used to run from Blonay to Clarens. (J.Wiseman)*

2.10. *On a wet day at Blonay as 0-6-0T no.6 prepares to depart for Chamby on 10th June 2001. On the far side of the station can be seen the rack and pinion tracks of the line to Les Pléiades. (D.Trevor Rowe)*

2.11.   This is another view of no.6 at Blonay, whilst shunting the rolling stock on 15th September 1974. The French influence in this part of Switzerland is reflected in the architecture of the station buildings. (J.K.Williams)

2.12.   2-6-0RT no.3 was similarly engaged at Blonay on 2nd September 1990. The impressive bulk of these splendid locomotives can be appreciated in this view.   (J.F.Organ)

2.13.   A final view of the Blonay-Chamby line as no.3 storms up the bank at Cornaux with the last train of the day on 2nd September 1990. (J.F.Organ)

2.14. One of the latest products of SLM, supplied in 1992. 0-4-2RT no.1 of the MTGN arrives at Caux, hauling a train on the descent from Rochers De Naye, in August 2000. (C.R.Stone)

2.16. Seen from the summit station at Rochers De Naye, 0-4-2RT no.1 was viewed approaching the "hairpin" avalanche shelter during the descent to Caux on 12th August 1997. The lower level of track can be seen behind the train. (D.Trevor Rowe)

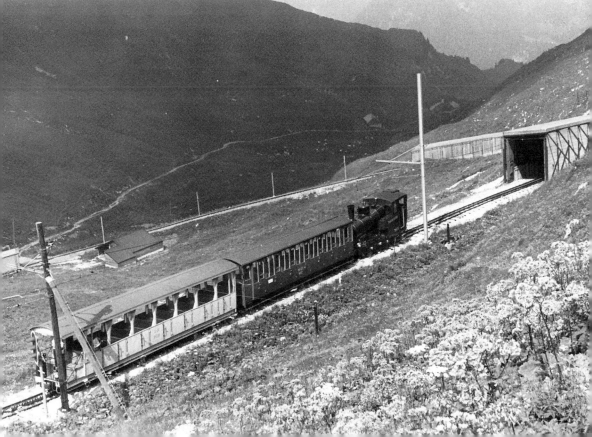

2.17.   One of the original diminutive electric locomotives built for the MTGN, dating from 1909, was photographed at Glion in August 1997. (D. Trevor Rowe)

2.18.   Portuguese 0-4-4-0T Mallet no. E 164, built by Henschel in 1905, is seen with a tourist train on the CF du Jura at Tavannes on 16th September 2001. This German locomotive looks quite at home in western Switzerland. (J. Wiseman)

2.19.   The other Mallet, 2-4-6-0T no. E 206 dating from 1913, was seen at Le Noirmont on 28th November 1993. Having spent its working life in Portugal, it is doubtful if this Henschel locomotive had ever operated in snow before! (J.Wiseman).

2.20.   Another view of Henschel no. E 206 is captured at Le Noirmont in November 1993. The CF de Jura operates a regular series of steam hauled trains, usually during the summer months. As can be seen, they also run occasionally during the winter. (J.Wiseman)

3. THE BERNESE OBERLAND

Interlaken, situated between Lake Thun and Lake Brienz, is the gateway to one of the most dramatic areas of scenic grandeur in the alpine regions. Overshadowed by the towering peaks of the Bernese Oberland with the Eiger, Mönch and Jungfrau dominating the scene, Interlaken Ost station is also the terminus of two contrasting metre gauge railways. The oldest of these is the *Bernese Oberland Bahn* (BOB) opened in 1890 and connects Interlaken with Lauterbrunnen and Grindelwald. The other is the SBB *Brünig* Line, which runs to another lakeside resort at Luzern. Although construction began at the Luzern end in 1888, the final link from Brienz to Interlaken wasn't completed until 1916. The BOB and SBB routes are rack and adhesion lines, whilst both connect with purely rack and pinion lines of 80cm gauge and one of these in turn connects with a metre gauge rack and pinion line that terminates at the highest railway station in Europe.

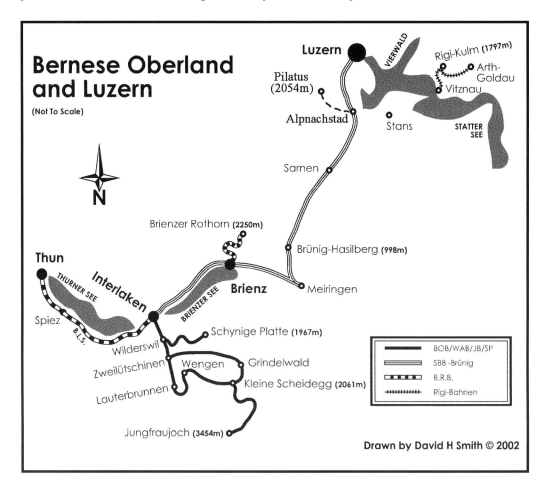

The Bernese Oberland Bahn

Following its opening on 1ˢᵗ July 1890, the metre gauge BOB was originally operated by steam locomotives. The rack and pinion sections utilise the Riggenbach system, which has a single rung "ladder" type of rack as opposed to the diagonally opposed twin tooth rack of the Abt system.

In common with most of the Swiss railway network, the BOB was electrified in March 1914, 1500 volts DC being utilised. The ultimate destiny of the steam locomotives is not recorded.

The BOB departs from Interlaken Ost in a sweeping curve towards Wilderswil, where a connection with the 80cm *Schynige Platte Bahn* is made. There then follows a run up the Lütschine Gorge to Zweilütschinen where the workshops and depot are situated. The line through the gorge was doubled in 1998 to allow an even more intensive service to operate. At Zweilütschinen the line divides, one route continuing south towards Lauterbrunnen and the other east towards Grindelwald. Both branches include two sections of rack and pinion before reaching their destinations, 12 and 19 km respectively from Interlaken.

Steam returned to the BOB in the early 1970s when former RhB 2-6-0T no.11 was purchased for the purpose of hauling occasional special excursions along the lower part of the route. As the SLM built locomotive, dating from 1908, is not fitted with rack equipment it is unable to reach the upper termini of the two branches. However, two of the original BOB electric machines are also preserved. These are able to ascend the rack sections in order that a journey along the entire route, with a combination of steam and electric traction, in the preserved vintage rolling stock can be enjoyed.

Schynige Platte Bahn

As mentioned above, the BOB connects with the SPB at Wilderswil. This 80cm line was opened in 1893 as an independent organisation to provide an easy access to the Alpine Garden at Schynige Platte from which superb views of the surrounding mountains and lakes can be seen in a perfect vista. The 1967m summit is reached by a 7.3 km Riggenbach line, which ascends the climb on a ruling gradient of 1 in 4.

Although it was constructed and originally operated by a separate concern, the SPB was taken over by the BOB in 1895. Steam power was used initially, the locomotives being the standard "kneeling cow" 0-4-2RT design produced by SLM with the boiler raked at a steep angle to compensate for the gradients. However, the line was electrified at the same period as the parent line was converted and the redundant locomotives sold to pastures new apart from one. The lone survivor is no.5, which was retained initially for engineering duties such as removing and replacing the catenary during the autumn and spring, the line being closed during the winter months.

As with so many other lines, the attraction of steam power was noted many years ago by the BOB management. Consequently, no.5 is in regular demand during the operating season when it propels a single coach up the incline with numerous special and charter workings. Even when the steam locomotive is not in use, the SPB retains its own appeal. Unique among Swiss mountain lines, the original 0-4-0 electric locomotives and rolling stock are still in regular use, modern two car units being conspicuous by their absence.

Wengernalpbahn

The two termini of the BOB at Lauterbrunnen and Grindelwald are linked by one of the most amazing railways in Europe. This is the 80cm *Wengernalpbahn* (WAB) which makes the connection via a summit at Kleine Scheidegg, situated at 2061m in the shadow of the North Face of the Eiger. The climb from Lauterbrunnen is 10.47 km in length with an average gradient of 1 in 5¼. When the line was opened in 1893, the first part of the ascent to Wengen was on a different route with a gradient of 1 in 4. A new route with an easier gradient was built in 1910, although the original alignment was retained for freight and works trains.

From the summit, the descent to Grund is by a 1 in 4 gradient. At Grund, where the workshops and depot are situated, a reversal is necessary before the short final steep climb to the terminus at Grindelwald, 8.64 km from Kleine Scheidegg is attained.

Like the SPB, the WAB is a Riggenbach rack and pinion line for its entire length and was originally operated by steam power. Although it has always retained its separate identity, the WAB is part of the BOB organisation and as such was electrified at an early stage of its life. However, unlike the SPB, none of the steam locomotives were retained and the electric units have been progressively updated during the last 90 years. Although some of the original 0-4-0 electric locomotives have been retained for engineering trains, and the occasional special working, the remainder were transferred to the SPB, which shares an identical power supply. It is regrettable that none of the steam locomotives were retained for such duties. The sight and sound of a steam propelled train working hard up the steep gradients of this most dramatic and scenic line would surely be a magnet for tourists and enthusiasts alike. Fortunately, one of the locomotives survived. It was transferred to the *Brienz-Rothorn-Bahn* in 1911, having been converted to the Abt system, where it remains in working order.

Kleine Scheidegg is also the lower terminus of a metre gauge railway fitted with the Strub rack system. The *Jungfrau Bahn* climbs for 9.3 km on a maximum gradient of 1 in 4, mainly in a tunnel. This has been cut through the rock of the Eiger and Mönch and terminates under the saddle of the Jungfraujoch. At 3454m (11,333ft), this is the highest railway station in Europe and was completed in 1912, construction having begun in 1896. Due to its largely underground route, the line was electrified from the start using a 3-phase 1125 volt 50Hz system. Although not a cheap railway on which to travel, the panoramic views from the observation platform on the Jungfraujoch are truly amazing - but pick the right day! The line also has two intermediate "stations" which have large plate glass windows cut into the rock face.

SBB Brünig Line

The only narrow gauge section of the SBB network, this 74 km line linking Interlaken and Luzern was constructed in stages between 1888 and 1916. The original stretch between Alpnachstad and Brienz, incorporating the Riggenbach rack sections over the Brünig pass, was built by the Jura-Bern-Luzern Railway (JBL) and opened on 14th June 1888. This was followed by the connection from Alpnachstad to Luzern 12 months later. In 1890 the enterprise was taken over by the Jura-Simplon (JS) concern, this being incorporated into the state system (SBB) in 1903. The final link between Brienz and Interlaken was finally completed on 23rd August 1916, so avoiding the need to transfer to a lake steamer for that leg of the journey.

Leaving Interlaken Ost, the line climbs steeply in order to cross the standard gauge sidings and the canalised River Aare which links Lake Thun and Lake Brienz. The route then runs alongside the northern side of Lake Brienz, passing through numerous short tunnels, until the first major station at Brienz is reached, 16 km from Interlaken. Here is situated the lower terminus of the *Brienz-Rothorn-Bahn* (BRB). If one chooses the right day, it is possible to see three different types of steam power at Brienz. Should a steam excursion be running on the Brünig line and the paddle steamer "Lötschberg" in operation on the lake, these combined with the rack and pinion steam locomotives of the BRB provide a fascinating spectacle.

Departing from Brienz the route continues to follow the lake and the wide Aare Valley until, after a further 13 km, Meiringen is reached. Here are situated the workshops and depot, and the major intermediate station of the line. Trains reverse at Meiringen and retrace their steps for about 1km until turning north and begin a climb on a 5 km 1in 9 rack section to the 996m.summit station at Brünig-Hasliberg. The descent to Giswil is split into three rack sections, mainly running through an area of woodland for 11km. The remaining 29 km to Luzern runs along the valley floor, via Alpnachstad where the lower terminus of the *Pilatus Bahn* is situated. This is the steepest rack and pinion line in Europe, with a gradient of 1 in 2 required to reach the 2054m. summit. The approach to Luzern is similar to that at Interlaken, with the metre gauge tracks climbing in order to pass over the maze of standard gauge sidings before dropping down into the western side of the SBB station.

The Brünig line was to remain steam operated until 1940-42, when it was electrified on the 15,000 volts AC system in common with the remainder of the SBB. Since 1990, the majority of trains have been hauled by a fleet of eight powerful HGe 4/4 11 Rack and Adhesion locomotives, which make light work of the steep gradients. The steam locomotives comprised of four basic types built by SLM between 1888 and 1926. For the adhesion only sections, 0-6-0Ts and 2-6-0Ts were employed whilst the remainder were 0-4-0RT and 0-6-0RT compound rack and adhesion machines. By 1926, a total of 36 steam locomotives were in use, equally split between adhesion types and those equipped for use on the rack sections. The 2-6-0Ts were joined in 1922 by four similar locomotives from the *Rhätische Bahn*, following the electrification of the RhB, whilst some of the former Jura-Simplon 0-6-0Ts were sold.

After the Brünig was modernised in 1942, most of the steam locomotives were sold abroad, the majority going to Greece. However, four have remained in Switzerland, two of which are preserved in working order. One of the 2-6-0Ts, no.208 built in 1913, is maintained at Meiringen and operates tourist and charter trains to Interlaken. The other locomotives are all 0-6-0RTs, one of which is in working order. This is no.1067 dating from 1910, which is used on excursions over the rack section to Giswil as well as the lower parts of the route. No.1067 has also made the occasional foray onto the BOB line. The other preserved locomotives are museum exhibits, no.1063 (built in 1909) being displayed in the Luzern Transport Museum whilst no.1068 (built in 1926) is mounted on a plinth at Meiringen station.

The two working locomotives are maintained and operated by an organisation known as "Friends of Steam locomotives, Meiringen" which was formed in 1965. This organisation has close links with the Ballenberg heritage museum, which has reconstructed historic buildings from throughout Switzerland on a site in delightful surroundings near Brienz.

Brienz-Rothorn-Bahn

This 7.6 km Abt system 80cm gauge rack and pinion railway climbs from Brienz to the 2250m. station at the Rothorn Kulm on a ruling gradient of 1 in 4. Construction began in 1890 and, following two years of continuous struggle against nature, opened in 1892. Unique among Swiss railways, the BRB was never electrified and steam reigned supreme until 1973, when diesel locomotives made their first appearance. Although not the highest terminal station in Switzerland, the BRB does have the distinction of surmounting the greatest difference in altitude between the 562m.lower station and summit.

Traffic declined dramatically during World War 1, despite the fact that Switzerland remained steadfastly neutral. As a result the line closed in 1915, which looked initially to be a permanent situation. However the track remained in position whilst the locomotives and rolling stock had been carefully stored at Brienz and the BRB eventually reopened in 1931. A further economic decline in the railway's fortunes occurred during the late 1950s, when maintenance costs were considerably more than operating profit. At the annual general meeting of the company in 1958, it was unanimously agreed that the line should be closed and replaced by a cable car system. However, the railway had many supporters who managed to overturn the decision. Following a period of considerable investment, the BRB was turned around into a very successful and efficient operation. The result is that the railway is one of the principal attractions in the Bernese Oberland, with a very secure future.

The steep climb begins abruptly from the station at Brienz, initially through woodland and meadows. There follows a series of tunnels, between which there are stunning glimpses of the lake below. The half way stage and watering point is at Planalp, a popular place for photography when as many as four trains are following each other up the mountain in a convoy system. The final climb to the summit is around a large horseshoe curve following the contours of the mountain, the terminus being reached after traversing a precipitous ledge and a final short tunnel.

Seven of the familiar SLM 0-4-2RT locomotives, built between 1891 and 1936, operate on the line alongside machinery of much later vintage. Of the five older locomotives, only nos. 2, 3 and 4 are original members of the stock. The current no.1 originally worked on the *Rochers-de-Naye* line until 1941 when it was transferred to the *Ferrovia Monte Generoso* on the Italian border. When the latter line abandoned steam power in 1962, it was transferred to the BRB to replace the withdrawn original no.1. No.5 is the sole surviving steam locomotive from the *Wengernalpbahn* from where it was transferred in 1911. Nos. 6 and 7 are of the later superheated version of the same design, delivered in 1933 and 1936 respectively.

In 1973 the first of four 0-4-0 diesel powered locomotives were delivered, along with some observation coaches with fully glazed roofs to a semi-circular profile. Despite these modern intrusions, the popularity of the steam locomotives remained the principal attraction of the line. This was confirmed in 1992 when SLM delivered the first of three, oil fired 0-4-2RT locomotives to a revolutionary design. These are numbered 12, 14 and 15, note the lack of no.13. As mentioned previously, another machine of the same design also works on the MTGN whilst some metre gauge examples have been supplied to Austria to work on the two ÖBB operated rack and pinion lines.

The BRB celebrated its centenary with much of its original equipment still operating alongside machinery of a much later vintage. The five locomotives dating from 1891/2 are now regarded as museum exhibits and consequently are treated with the respect they deserve. However the more powerful machines built in 1933/6 work alongside the three modern additions and the four diesels. The sight and sound of the powerful rack and pinion steam locomotives pounding up the 1 in 4 gradients, propelling two fully laden carriages, is an unforgettable experience.

3.1. *Former RhB 2-6-0T no.11, now fitted with air braking in order to be compatible with the rolling stock at its new home, was captured at Interlaken Ost prior to working a wedding train to Wilderswil on the* **Bernese Oberland Bahn** *(BOB) in June 1983. (C.R.Stone)*

3.2. *SPB 0-4-2RT no.5 at Wilderswil is about to depart to Schynige Platte with a special charter train in June 1983. Apart from being fitted with Riggenbach rack equipment, this locomotive is identical to the contemporary Abt fitted locomotives on the BRB. (C.R.Stone)*

3.3.   A train from Schynige Platte arrives at Wilderswil behind one of the original electric locomotives, supplied in 1914, on 20th September 1988. Unique among Swiss narrow gauge lines, the SPB still relies on vintage equipment for all its trains. (J.F.Organ)

3.4.   An early view of a steam propelled train ascending the Schynige Platte Bahn is from the first decade of the 20th century. The view includes Lake Thun and the Neisen. Interlaken is out of sight behind the high ground between the locomotive and lake. (K.Taylorson coll.)

3.5.   Dating from the early years of electrification of the SPB, this archive view shows a train ascending the climb with the Jungfrau dominating the scene. (K.Taylorson coll.)

3.6.   The summit station at Schynige Platte was photographed in July 1981. The beautiful surroundings of this mountain terminus, from where superb views of the mountains are to be enjoyed, can be appreciated in this view. (J.Marsh)

3.7.   A rare view features a steam propelled train ascending the **Wengernalpbahn** *at the turn of the 20th century. Once again the Jungfrau dominates the skyline, whilst the locomotive appears to be similar to the first batch of Snowdon engines built in 1895. (K.Taylorson coll.)*

3.8.   A 1500 volts DC electric two car unit approaches Wengen in February 1985 with a crowded train of winter sports enthusiasts. The open truck being propelled by the train contains innumerable pairs of skis, which presumably can be identified by their rightful owners! (J.F.Organ)

3.9.   A busy scene was recorded at Kleine Scheidegg, the mid-point station where the two sections of the WAB converge. An electric railcar and trailer coach prepares to leave for Lauterbrunnen in February 1985. (J.F.Organ)

3.10.   0-6-0RT no.1055 is at work on the SBB Brünig line during the 1930s. This 1906 built locomotive was sold to the Thessaly Railway in Greece in 1949, and is currently reported to be in store at Volos. (J.K.Williams coll.)

3.11.   2-6-0T no.208 prepares to depart from Interlaken Ost with a train bound for Meiringen on 20th September 1988. The vintage rolling stock is a mixture of SBB and BOB vehicles, the latter being marshalled immediately behind the locomotive. (J.F.Organ)

3.12.   No.208 presents a superb sight as it waits in the passing loop at Neiderried, between Interlaken and Brienz, on 21st September 1988. (J.F.Organ)

3.13.   Sister locomotive no.218 leaves Brienz with a train bound for Interlaken during the latter days of regular steam haulage on the Brünig line during the late 1930s. (J.K.Williams coll.)

3.14. *The superbly preserved no.208 arrives at Brienz with one of the special trains that operated during 1988. These trains are a regular occurrence on the SBB Brünig section with either 2-6-0T no.208 or 0-6-0RT no.1067 used for these duties. (J.F.Organ).*

3.15. *A view of Brienz station in the 1920s includes 2-6-0T no.215 as it collects passengers before continuing the journey from Interlaken to Meiringen. (J.K.Williams coll.)*

3.16. *On 20th September 1988, the scene at Brienz had changed little since the previous photograph was taken. No.208 arrives with a train from Meiringen in an almost timeless scene. (J.F.Organ)*

3.17. A final view of no.208 shows it as its runs around the train that it has hauled from Interlaken. The arrangement during 1988 was a morning round trip to Brienz followed by an afternoon return journey to Meiringen. (J.F.Organ)

3.18. Many Swiss locomotives were sold to Greece during the 1940s. Former SBB 2-6-0Ts nos.205 and 204 are seen in store at Volos on 13th May 1961. (D.Trevor Rowe)

3.19. An immaculate 0-6-0RT no.1067 waits at Brünig-Hasliberg whilst working a special train from Giswil to Meiringen in September 1996. (C.R.Stone)

3.20. No.1067 is on the turntable at Giswil, earlier the same afternoon. The diminutive engine shed, which used to house a banking locomotive, is of a most unusual design. (C.R.Stone)

3.21. An atmospheric view features no.1067 as it departs amid clouds of steam for Meiringen from Brünig-Hasliberg in September 1996. (C.R.Stone)

3.22. **Brienz-Rothorn-Bahn** *0-4-2RT no.4 leaves Brienz with a train bound for Rothorn Kulm on 21st September 1988. This is one of the original locomotives delivered to the BRB in 1892 and is propelling one of the new coaches supplied in 1987. (J.F.Organ)*

3.23.   On the same occasion, BRB no.6 built in 1933 prepares to depart from Brienz for a climb up the mountain. The immaculate condition of the BRB locomotives is clearly shown in this view. (J.F.Organ)

3.24.   Here is a rare view of the front end of BRB no.7, delivered in 1936. Normally this view isn't possible due to the locomotives propelling their coaches up the line. The gearing below the smokebox connecting the piston rods to the rack motion is clearly seen. (J.K.Williams coll.)

3.25. *Built 1891 and still working hard, 0-4-2RT no.2 propels one of the observation coaches delivered in 1973, shortly after leaving Brienz on 16th August 1977. (J.Wiseman)*

3.26. *On the same date, no.7 propels two coaches comprising a bogie vehicle and a four-wheeled coach through the alpine meadows of the lower section of the climb. (J.Wiseman)*

3.27. *0-4-2RT no.6 attacks the lower section of the climb to the summit in August 1961. The reason for the steeply inclined boiler can be appreciated in this view. (J.K.Williams coll.)*

3.28. *A panoramic view of the surrounding mountains is seen in this scene as one of the later locomotives departs from the mid-way station at Planalp during the 1950s. (J.K.Williams coll.)*

3.29. *On the final part of the climb, no.6 is seen below Rothorn on 30th August 1987. Note the guard on the balcony of the leading coach with the handbrake close to hand. (J.Wiseman)*

3.30. A dramatic scenic backdrop adds to this superb view of 0-4-2RT no.6 as it approaches the summit in August 1987. The views from the train are equally impressive, with panoramic vistas of Lake Brienz and the surrounding mountains. (J.Wiseman)

4. ZERMATT to DISENTIS

Europe's most famous narrow gauge rail service, the "Glacier Express" completes the 290km journey between Zermatt and St.Moritz in less than 8 hours. Hauled by powerful electric locomotives, light work is made of the severe gradients along the route, many of which include sections of rack and pinion. Three independent railway companies are involved in the joint operation, two of which incorporate the above mentioned rack sections. These are the *Brig-Visp-Zermatt Bahn* (BVZ), the *Furka-Oberalp-Bahn* (FO) and the *Rhätische Bahn* (RhB), the latter eschewing rack assistance for its extensive system. In view of its size and importance, the RhB will be covered in a separate chapter. However, in view of their close working relationship, the BVZ and FO will be linked together for the purpose of this publication.

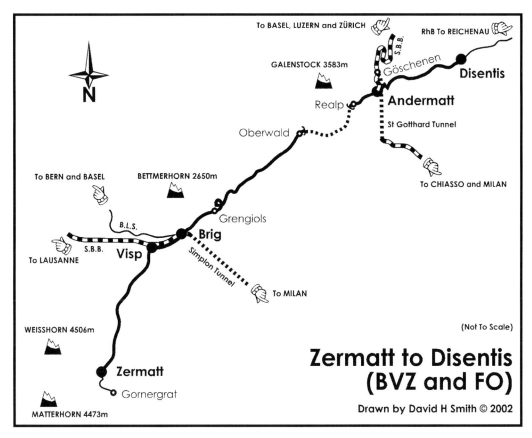

Zermatt to Disentis (BVZ and FO)

Drawn by David H Smith © 2002

(Not To Scale)

Brig-Visp-Zermatt Bahn

Opened in 1891, the 36 km *Visp-Zermatt Bahn* (VZ) was constructed to link Zermatt, at the foot of the Matterhorn, with the Rhône Valley at Visp. The route incorporates six sections of the Abt system of rack and pinion with a ruling gradient of 1 in 8. The line follows the valley of the Matter-Visp as it descends from Zermatt, passing through Täsch, Randa, Herbriggen, St.Niklaus and Stalden before reaching Visp. The most impressive section is that through the Kipfen Gorge near St.Niklaus, where the line is in close proximity to the rapids and torrents of the river. In 1991 a huge landslide near Herbriggen buried a section of the railway, necessitating the construction of a 3km diversionary route incorporating a new rack and pinion section.

Until 1929, the independent railway was operated by steam locomotives, ten 0-4-2RTs built by SLM for the opening of the line. In 1930, the 9 km extension along the Rhône Valley to Brig was completed, thereby allowing a physical connection with the *Furka-Oberalp Bahn* (FO). At this time, the 45 km *Brig-Visp-Zermatt Bahn* (BVZ) as it had become, was electrified at 11,000 volts AC 16.7Hz, in common with the FO and RhB. At the same time the steam locomotives were replaced by five HGe 4/4 "Crocodile" type electric locomotives, nos. 11-16. In more recent years these historic locomotives have been supplemented with modern machines, such as the powerful HGe 4/4 11 design, five of which were introduced in 1990. However the faithful "Crocodiles" remain in service, used mainly on freight trains and the occasional special working.

The steam locomotives were subsequently withdrawn and sold, apart from two. Nos. 6 and 7 were retained for emergency and engineering duties, and subsequently found a new niche by hauling tourist and charter steam hauled excursions. No.7 is currently based at Brig, whilst no.6 has been transferred to the "new" Furka Mountain Line - of which more in due course.

The connection with the FO at Brig allowed through running between the BVZ and RhB, and so was born the idea of the "Glacier Express" linking the two winter sports centres of Zermatt and St.Moritz, in addition to the intermediate towns of Brig, Andermatt, Disentis and Chur.

As Zermatt is a dedicated "traffic free area", apart from a battery powered bus service, electric luggage carriers and horse drawn taxis, a large car park has been created at Täsch from where a regular shuttle service operates over the upper 6km of the route. This intensive service provides a valuable income for the BVZ whilst passengers can enjoy the stunning scenery with the unique and incomparable Matterhorn dominating the skyline to the south. Zermatt is also the lower terminus of the *Gornergratbahn,* a metre gauge rack and pinion line opened in 1898. This 10 km line that is operated on a 725 volt 5oHz three-phase system, terminates at the highest open-air station in Europe at the 3070m Gornergrat.

Furka-Oberalp-Bahn

In 1910 a company known as the "*Brig-Furka-Disentis*"(BFD) was formed with the intention of linking Brig to Disentis, the western terminus of the RhB. With the backing of French capital and engineering expertise, construction of the upper section of the line between Gletsch and Disentis, via Andermatt, was begun during 1911 and 1912. Considering the terrain of the route, this was a very expensive and difficult route to construct, including numerous rack and pinion sections combined with spiral and hairpin tunnels.

Two years later, the link between Brig and Gletsch was completed but the outbreak of World War 1 resulted in a complete halt of further work. With the French promoters otherwise engaged, the BFD continued to provide a service on the lower section of the route whilst attempting to complete work on the incomplete "mountain" sections. The inevitable result was the BFD going into receivership in 1923 and the dream of a railway link between the Rhône and Rhine appeared to be at an end. However a consortium mainly comprised by directors of the VZ and RhB bought the assets of the BFD in 1925 and reformed the company as the *Furka-Oberalp-Bahn.* Their first task was to complete the construction of the route, the line opening between Brig and Disentis in 1926.

With the completion of the BVZ route between Brig and Visp in 1930, it was finally possible to make the 290 km journey between Zermatt and St.Mortitz. In addition it was also possible to continue a further 60 km beyond St.Moritz to Tirano in Italy via the tracks of the *Bernina Bahn.* However the entire journey was only possible in summer, when the difficult route over the Furka Pass was clear of snow.

Situated in the square outside the SBB station, the joint BVZ/FO station at Brig is the terminus of the two lines. In order to continue the journey between Zermatt and Disentis, the train reverses before turning sharply onto the FO tracks. After crossing the Rhône and passing under the standard gauge tracks, the FO route continues via Grengiols, Fiesch and Münster to Oberwald. At Grengiols is the first rack section, where the line climbs through a spiral tunnel in order to reach the plateau known as The Goms. From Oberwald the original route climbed 490 metres through a further spiral tunnel before arriving at Gletsch, in the shadow of the Rhône Glacier. From Gletsch, the relentless climb on a 1 in 9 gradient continued to the 2160m. Furka Summit Tunnel before the equally steep descent to Realp. This last section included the famous Steffenbach Bridge spanning a side valley notorious for avalanches. For this reason, the bridge was designed to be dismantled during the winter, the main span being pushed back beyond the abutments by means of a gantry and winches incorporated into the design.

The section between Oberwald and Realp could never be used between October and June, due to the amount of snow and danger of avalanches. In order to provide a year round service on the FO route, a 16km base tunnel was constructed between 1973 and 1982, which resulted in the abandonment of the Furka Pass route. The result was a decrease in journey times of almost an hour between Brig and Disentis.

The descent from Realp to Andermatt is far less severe, running through a wide glacial valley. At Andermatt there is a junction with a branch to Göschenen, where a connection is made with the SBB at the northern end of the Gotthard tunnel. This 3.7 km line with a gradient of 1 in 5½ was originally a separate concern known as the *Schöllenen Bahn,* opened in 1917 and absorbed by the FO in 1960.

Immediately after leaving Andermatt station, the FO resumes the climb on the rack at 1 in 9 through a series of hairpin tunnels to the summit at Oberalppasshöhe, an altitude of 2033m. Unlike the Furka Pass, the section over the Oberalp Pass was able to remain open throughout the year due to the number of tunnels and avalanche shelters protecting the line from the worst of the elements. The final descent to Disentis, via Tschamut-Selva and Sedrun includes further sections of rack and pinion. The entry to the station at Disentis, overshadowed by the huge Benedictine Abbey, is made through a short tunnel under the town. Here the FO makes an "end on" connection with the RhB.

The original locomotives of the BFD, later acquired by the FO, were ten powerful 2-6-0RTs constructed by SLM in 1913. These 42 tonne 600 hp rack and adhesion compound machines could haul loads of 60 tonnes with a maximum speed of 45 kph on the adhesion sections and 20 kph on the rack. These impressive locomotives provided the motive power on the FO until 1942 when electrification was completed. Two locomotives, nos.3 and 4, were retained for emergency and engineering purposes, the remainder being sold. These went to French Indo-China, now known as Vietnam, where they continued in use until that country was torn apart by the conflicts during the 1960s. Prior to the opening of the Furka Base Tunnel, a regular duty of nos. 3 and 4 was pushing a huge wedge plough to clear the snow from the route between Oberwald and Realp during the early months of spring.

Following electrification, seven HGe 4/4 locomotives derived from the BVZ "Crocodiles" were supplied by SLM between 1940 and 1956. These historic machines are notable for their open balconies in front of the cabs at each end, in place of the sloping bonnets of the BVZ design. Although still in service, they are now used on lesser duties, their use on the premier trains being replaced by the eight powerful HGe 4/4 11 locomotives, identical to those supplied to the BVZ and Brünig line, which were delivered between 1986 and 1989.

Following the closure of the Furka Pass route in 1982, the future of SLM 2-6-0RT no.4 appeared in doubt. Although both locomotives had been used for occasional special charter trains in addition to their snow clearing duties, no.3 had been sold to the Blonay-Chamby line in 1970. Following an extensive overhaul, this is now a regular performer at its new home, even though the rack equipment is no longer required. No.4 remained at Brig, until being "retired" to a shed at Münster in the anticipation of being required for future duties. Fortunately, these "duties" are soon to present themselves from an unexpected source.

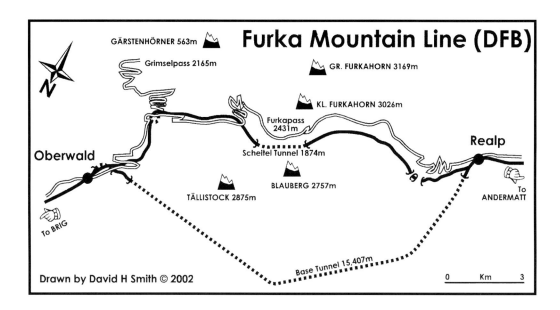

Dampfbahn Furka-Bergstrecke

Following the opening of the Furka Base Tunnel in 1982 and the subsequent closure of the route over the Furka Pass, a preservation group was formed with the intention of saving this section of line. By December 1983, a company to be known as *Dampfbahn Furka-Bergstrecke* (DFB) or Furka Steam Mountain Railway had been formed and was in active discussions with the FO and local government with regard to its proposals.

By 1985 work had begun at Gletsch, where the station was restored as an information bureau, and at Realp where a workshop and depot was created. Former BVZ 0-4-2RT no.6 was purchased along with an industrial diesel whilst work on rebuilding the track on the eastern flank of the pass was progressing well. Suitable rolling stock was also acquired from various locations in Switzerland. One consolation of the continuous modernisation of the Swiss railway network is the availability of redundant rolling stock in excellent condition. 1988 was to be a milestone year. The Steffenbach Bridge was reinstalled whilst further from home, four of the 2-6-0RT locomotives were traced in Vietnam and subsequently repatriated.

1989 saw the first public trains ascend the incline, initially as far as the Steffenbach Bridge and subsequently extended to Tiefenbach in 1992. Meanwhile the repatriated locomotives (nos. 1, 2, 8 and 9) were despatched to Germany for restoration whilst an agreement with the FO for the long-term loan of no.4 was arranged. Part of this agreement was that the DFB would be responsible for restoring and maintaining the locomotive in working order.

By 1997, trains were running again through the summit tunnel as far as Muttbach-Belvédère, where superb views of the Rhône Glacier can be enjoyed. The following year, services were extended to Gletsch, which is currently the western terminus. The remainder of the route through the spiral tunnel to Oberwald has been partially obliterated by a road improvement scheme. Work is now proceeding on rebuilding this section of line, incorporating a new alignment where necessary.

Two of the locomotives acquired from Vietnam returned to service in 1993. The first to be restored were former FO nos.1 and 2, now renumbered DFB nos.1 and 2 respectively. No.9 was returned to service by 2000, with no.8 to follow in due course. The former BVZ loco no.6 has retained its original identity, having been overhauled in Chur. FO no.4 has since been despatched to Chur for similar treatment. During their "sabbatical" in the Far East the 2-6-0RTs were fitted with extended coal bunkers behind the cabs. This feature was retained when the locomotives were restored in Germany.

Another interesting steam powered machine acquired by the DFB is the former RhB rotary snowplough no.9212, which is based at Gletsch. This fascinating machine was obtained from the Blonay-Chamby in exchange for RhB no.9214. Although similar in appearance, no.9214 is self-propelled, being driven by a Meyer type locomotive chassis. On 9212, the boiler and cylinders only provide power to the snowplough mechanism, the unit requiring to be propelled by another locomotive. Due to the overall condition of the boiler and other mechanical components, no.9212 was deemed to be a better candidate for restoration to working condition. Both snowploughs were built by SLM in 1912, along with another self-propelled example no.9213, which has been retained by the RhB.

Even though the project is still incomplete, the DFB must rank as one of the finest tourist railways in Europe. With a combination of unsurpassed scenery, powerful locomotives working hard and Swiss efficiency, this is railway preservation at its finest. Due to the terrain, services can only operate between late June and early October. It is also fairly expensive at 93 Swiss Francs (£37.20) for the 32 km return journey between Realp and Gletsch, but no doubt worth every penny, especially if the weather is kind!

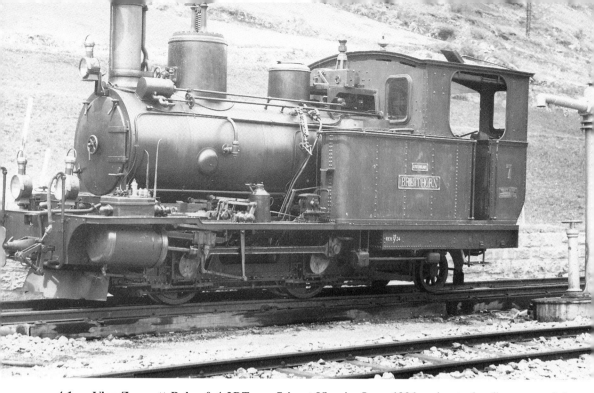

4.1. **Visp-Zermatt-Bahn** *0-4-2RT no. 7 is at Visp in June 1981, prior to hauling a special excursion through the beautiful valley to Zermatt. These locomotives were deceptively powerful, despite their relatively small size. (J.K.Williams)*

4.2. **Sister** *locomotive no.6, on loan from the Furka Mountain Railway, departs from Visp with a VZ centenary special train bound for Zermatt on 20th October 1991. (J.Wiseman)*

4.3.   *No.7 at Herbriggen waits for a service train to pass, whilst hauling another special train on 29th May 1967. (D.Trevor Rowe)*

4.4.   *Continuing its ascent of the BVZ, no.7 pauses at Randa for another service stop on the same occasion. (D.Trevor Rowe)*

4.5. *The dramatic Kipfen Gorge is seen from a Zermatt bound train in September 1989. The motive power is an articulated twin railcar unit. (J.F.Organ)*

4.6. *0-4-2RT no.7 arrives at Zermatt with a train from Brig on 13th October 1991. This train and the one shown in photograph 4.2, formed part of the centenary celebrations of the VZ. (J.Wiseman)*

4.7.   One of the VZ "Crocodile" electric locomotives, supplied in 1929, was captured at Brig station in February 1988. No.12 had just arrived from Zermatt hauling a passenger train, although by that time their use was mainly confined to freight duties. (J.F.Organ)

4.8.   Furka-Oberalp-Bahn 2-6-0RT no.10 replenishes its water tanks at Brig depot on 15th January 1932. This locomotive, along with most of its compatriots, was exported to the Far East in the late 1940s. No.10 wasn't among those repatriated in 1989 and is probably still lurking in a Vietnamese jungle! (F.Ward/J.K.Williams coll.)

4.9.   A trio of Furka-Oberalp HGe 4/4 electric locomotives, with their distinctive end balconies were at Brig depot on 29th May 1967. Between 1942 and 1986, these historic machines were responsible for hauling the principle passenger trains on the FO. (D.Trevor Rowe)

4.10.   HGe 4/4 11 no.107 has just arrived at Brig Station on 18th September 1989. These rack and adhesion electric units, supplied in the 1980s, are the most powerful metre gauge locomotives in Europe. Examples are also at work on the BVZ and SBB Brünig line. (J.F.Organ)

4.11.   2-6-0RT no.4 waits in a passing loop near Grengiols on 28th May 1967 with a single coach special train. Note the lifting jack above the left-hand cylinder. *(D. Trevor Rowe)*

4.12.   No.4 departs from the loop on the same occasion with a gathering of spectators - and not a camera in sight! *(D. Trevor Rowe)*

4.13. *Further up the Goms plateau, no.4 approaches Ulrichen with its lightweight train. The reason for this special working is not recorded, probably connected with a track inspection rather than a charter train. (D.Trevor Rowe)*

4.14. *FO 2-6-0RT no. 2 was at Oberwald in 1930 complete with a snowplough. For the annual snow clearance on the upper reaches of the Furka Pass, a much larger, independent, wedge plough was propelled by a steam locomotive. Following electrification in 1942, the electric catenary was dismantled during the winter months to avoid being damaged by heavy snow falls and avalanches. (BVA coll.)*

4.15. *A view of Gletsch in 1915 has the Rhône Glacier prominent in the background. At that time, this was the eastern terminus of the* **Brig-Furka-Disentis (BFD)**, *as it was then known.* *(J.L.Rochaix coll./BVA)*

4.16. *59 years later at Gletsch, note how the Glacier has receded over the ensuing years. A HGe 4/4 prepares to depart with a train for Brig on 27th July 1974. (J.L.Rochaix/BVA)*

4.17. On the same occasion, a train departs from Gletsch, on the steep climb to the summit tunnel, bound for Disentis. The locomotive is one of the combined motor car and luggage vans, which are still in service on local trains. (J.L.Rochaix/BVA)

←⎯⎯⎯⎯⎯⎯

4.18. One of the 2-6-0RTs begins the rack-assisted ascent from Gletsch to the Furka Summit Tunnel in 1925. In the background is the Grimsel Pass, which climbs over the mountains to Meiringen. (VHS coll./BVA)

4.19.   2-6-0RT no.4 makes a fine sight as it storms up the incline towards the tunnel, having just cleared the rack section. The "A" board denoting the start of the rack and pinion can be seen to the rear of the last coach. A clearer view of the Grimsel Pass can be seen in this photograph, captured on 28th September 1968. (J.Wiseman)

4.20.   Steam returns to the Furka. A scene on the **Dampfbahn Furka-Bergstrecke (DFB)** as 2-6-0RT no.9 arrives at Gletsch during an off season blizzard on 16th September 2001. The extended coal- bunker fitted during the locomotive's sojourn in the Far East is clearly seen in this view. (R.Elkin)

4.21. Bedecked with flowers, no.9 prepares to depart from Gletsch with the return working to Realp. The blizzard had eased at that moment but intensified again a few minutes later. (R.Elkin)

4.22. Repatriated 2-6-0RT no.2 replenishes its water tanks at Tiefenbach during the climb from Realp to the summit in July 1994. At that time trains were only running as far as the Furka Pass tunnel. (N.Britton)

4.23. *Empty stock enters Realp station on a damp morning in July 1994, hauled by no.2. The entrance to the FO "Furka Base Tunnel" can be seen behind the train. The old route, which has been restored by the DFB, curves to the right alongside the tunnel portal. (N.Britton)*

4.24. *HGe 4/4 11 no.103 arrives at Disentis, with an afternoon Glacier Express bound for St. Moritz, on 27th September 1989. The FO locomotive will hand over to a RhB machine for the remainder of the journey. (J.F.Organ)*

5. DIE RHÄTISCHE BAHN

This extensive 375 km system in the Grisons, which is the largest of the privately operated railways in Switzerland, is effectively a metre gauge main line network. The original section was opened in 1889 between Landquart and Klosters, with an extension to Davos completed the following year. At Landquart, a connection was made with the standard gauge route between Zurich and Chur. The 51km *Landquart-Davos-Bahn* was extended a further 19 km in 1909 to Filisur where it connected with the *Albula-Bahn.* The latter was built between 1896 and 1904 to link Landquart, Chur and St.Moritz, a total distance of 103 km. Although initiated by separate concerns, the two projects were merged in 1895 to form The *Rhätische Bahn* (RhB) or Rhaetian Railway.

Subsequent extensions included the 49 km branch along the Rhine Valley from Reichenau (on the Albula line) to Disentis in 1912 and the 52 km Engadine branch from Samedan, near St.Moritz, to Schuls-Tarasp in 1913. Plans were in hand to extend the latter line over the Austrian border to connect with the Arlberg Railway at Landeck. However the events of 1914 prevented this being achieved, although the proposal has been constantly discussed during the last 80 years. It is quite probable that this connection could finally be achieved during the next decade, especially since the opening in 1999 of the 19 km Vereina tunnel between Klosters and Sagliains, near Schuls-Tarasp.

Two independent railways, which were ultimately absorbed by the RhB, were opened in 1910 and 1914. These were the *Bernina Bahn* and the *Chur-Arosa Bahn* respectively, both of which were taken over in 1942. In the same year, the RhB also took over the isolated *Bellinzona-Mesocco Bahn,* situated in the south of the country near the Italian border.

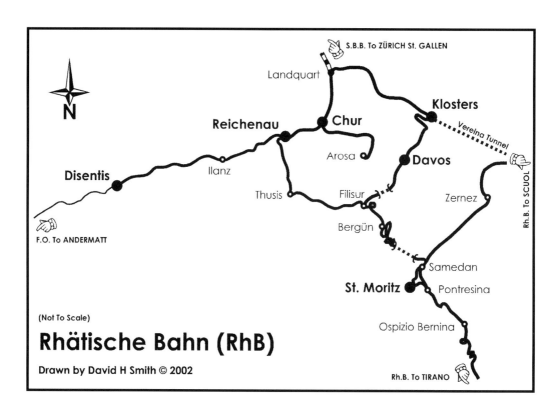

Rhätische Bahn (RhB)

(Not To Scale)

Drawn by David H Smith © 2002

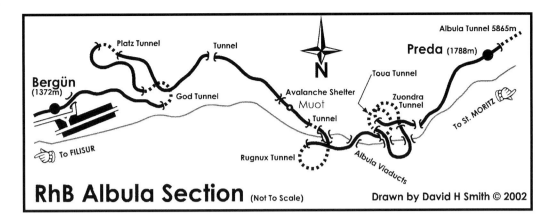

RhB Albula Section (Not To Scale)   Drawn by David H Smith © 2002

The Bernina line was built from St.Moritz to Tirano in Italy, where it connects with the Italian State Railway line to Milan. This 61km highly scenic route was electrified from the outset on a 1000 volts DC system. With gradients of 1 in 14 it is one of the steepest adhesion railways in Europe, the route also includes the highest surface railway crossing of the Alps at 2257m. Other outstanding features are the hairpin tunnels on the descent from Alp Grüm to Poschiavo and the spiral viaduct at Brusio. The final 4km from Campocologno to Tirano is actually on Italian soil although the customs point is in fact at Tirano station.

The Arosa line was also electrified from the start using a 2400 volts DC system. The 26km route with maximum gradients of 1 in 17 departs from Chur in the square outside the station, similar to the arrangement at Brig. The first 2 km pass through the streets of this historic town, before ascending the Plessur valley via numerous viaducts and tunnels to the winter sports centre of Arosa. The largest civil engineering feature of the route is the 287 metre ferro-concrete Langwies viaduct including a main span of 100m, which crosses the Plessur 62m. above the river.

The two original sections of the RhB network possess highly scenic sections incorporating extensive civil engineering features. Following a fairly gentle climb from Landquart to Klosters, the route to Davos climbs steeply on a curvaceous gradient of 1 in 22, including a hairpin tunnel at Cavadürli. From Davos, the route descends through the narrow Landwasser valley via a series of tunnels, between which there are fleeting glimpses of the gorge, before emerging at Wiesen. The line then crosses the 210 metre Wiesen Viaduct, 88m above the river. A footpath is also incorporated in the viaduct, precariously attached to the top of the structure alongside the track. Finally the line drops down to Filisur, which is entered on a sharp curve.

However it is the Albula line which is renowned world wide as being one of the finest railway routes in Europe. Following the climb from the Rhine valley at Reichenau to Thusis, the mountains close in dramatically as the line climbs through the Albula valley. Shortly before Filisur, the famous Landwasser Viaduct is crossed. The 130 metre six arch curving structure, carries the line 65m above the Landwasser river before it plunges into a tunnel high up on the precipitous rock face. After connecting with the Davos line at Filisur, there begins a climb on a ruling gradient of 1 in 29 via Bergün and the world famous Albula spirals to Preda. This section includes two hairpin and three spiral tunnels plus four major viaducts, interspersed with numerous smaller structures, in the 21km ascent from Filisur to the 5866m. long Albula tunnel between Preda and Spinas. The 1823m summit of the line is passed during the passage of the tunnel. The route then descends to Bever Junction, where the Engadine line is joined shortly before the major junction of Samedan is reached. From here the route divides, the right hand branch curving towards St. Moritz whilst the main line proceeds to Pontresina and a connection with the Bernina line. This 5 km "cut off" line was constructed to enable through running between the Albula and Bernina lines, avoiding the need to reverse at St.Moritz.

The majority of the original RhB was originally operated by steam haulage. However, when the Engadine branch was constructed in 1913 it was electrified at 11,000 volts AC 16.7Hz as a "test bed" for future modernisation. The success of the project resulted in the remainder of the RhB system being converted to electric operation between 1919 and 1922. When the Bernina and Arosa lines were absorbed in 1942, sections with three different power outputs were included in the network. In order to allow a speedy transfer of motive power between the Albula and Bernina routes, the station layout at Pontresina contains a complex mixture of AC and DC electrical equipment. At St.Moritz, the two routes are isolated in separate sections of the station. The same applied at Chur, with the Arosa line situated outside the station, although there is a connecting track for stock transfer purposes. This connection crosses the standard gauge tracks of the SBB, Chur being a joint station shared by the RhB and State system. In 1991 the Arosa line was converted to 11,000 AC in order to allow through running. It was intended to replace the street section of the line through Chur with an underground route, but this plan appears to have been postponed indefinitely.

The main workshops and depot of the RhB are located at Landquart, whilst sub-depots are also located at Chur and Samedan on the main RhB sections, plus Pontresina and Poschiavo on the Bernina line. The Samedan depot also includes extensive workshop facilities. The Landquart works is a very extensive complex, and is one of the principal centres of employment in the area.

Motive Power of the RhB

When the first section of the network was opened in 1889, the original locomotives were 2-6-0Ts built by SLM. Ultimately, sixteen of these relatively small machines were supplied between 1889 and 1908. However, it soon became obvious that more powerful locomotives would be required in view of the steep gradients on the higher sections of the system. Consequently, in 1891 the first of twelve Mallet tanks were supplied. These were delivered in three batches until 1902. The first two, nos.21 and 22, were 0-4-4-0Ts, followed in 1896 by a further two, nos.23 and 24 incorporating a trailing axle as 0-4-4-2Ts. The final eight arrived in 1902 with a leading pony truck replacing the trailing axle. These 2-4-4-0Ts, nos. 25 to 32 were the most successful variation of the design. However, with increasing loads to haul up the steeply graded routes, even more powerful locomotives were required. The result was that SLM supplied twenty-nine 2-8-0 tender engines between 1904 and 1915. These were based on a standard gauge design that had been successfully used by the SBB. Numbered 101 to 129, the first six were a 2 cylinder compound design whilst the remainder were superheated locomotives with two simple cylinders.

Following the initial electrification schemes in 1913, a variety of electric locomotives were delivered until a successful design was accepted. These were the fifteen Ge 6/6 "Crocodiles", nos. 401-415, supplied between 1921 and 1929, some of which are still in service today.

In 1947, a massive modernisation programme was begun. The first locomotives to be supplied in this scheme were ten Ge 4/4 (BoBo) locomotives, which were in effect metre gauge versions of the Re 4/4 standard gauge machines. These were followed in 1958 by the first of seven Ge 6/6 11 articulated locomotives mounted on three bogies (BoBoBo), the articulation of the bodywork being in a vertical plane to allow for the sudden changes of gradient. Between 1973 and 1983, a class of Ge 4/4 11 locomotives were supplied by SLM. These Thyristor controlled machines, nos.611 to 633, are closely based on the SBB Re 4/4 11 standard gauge design. They were joined in 1992 by the first of an updated version of the same design, known as the Ge 4/4 111. In conjunction with the delivery of the latest locomotives, the older Ge 4/4s were extensively refurbished at Landquart. This involved equipping them for push-pull operation on the Arosa line, following its conversion to 11,000 volts AC.

Both the Bernina line and the Arosa branch, prior to its conversion, have relied on railcar units rather than locomotive hauled trains. However the *Bernina Bahn,* in its independent period, possessed two larger locomotives, a Ge 6/6 no.81, built in 1916, and a Ge 4/4 "Crocodile" no.82, dating from 1928. These were renumbered 181 and 182 following their being absorbed into the RhB stock. No.81 was rebuilt as a Ge 4/4 in 1929, following the success of 82. This locomotive has been restored by the Blonay-Chamby, where it has resided since 1970. No.182 has retained its original design, and remained in service until 1976. Following five years on display at the Luzern Transport Museum, it was transferred to the *CFT de La Mure* in the French Alps with the intention of it being restored for use on tourist trains on that scenic route. Due to incompatibility of the electrical equipment, this proved to be not possible. In 1999, no.182 returned to its native soil in the care of a preservation group based at Poschiavo. Their intention is to restore the historic locomotive to working order. As a replacement for the Bernina locomotives, two Gem 4/4 locomotives, nos.801and 802, equipped with diesel engines in addition to their 1000 volts DC equipment, were supplied in 1968. Normally allocated to the Bernina line, they have occasionally appeared on the main system during an emergency.

Following the completion of the electrification of the RhB in 1922, the steam locomotives became redundant and were gradually sold. Three of the 2-6-0Ts remain in Switzerland. No.1 returned to its former home in 1989, following two decades at the Blonay-Chamby, where it had been restored. No.11, following many years service on the RhB, was sold to the BOB in 1970, whilst no.14 works on the *Appenzeller Bahn* in northern Switzerland. The remainder of the 2-6-0Ts were scattered far and wide to destinations such as Luxembourg, Italy, Spain, Brazil and Greece. The latter were among the four locomotives transferred to the SBB for service on the Brünig line, which ultimately sold many of its steam locomotives for service on the Thessaly Railway in Greece.

The Mallets were equally well distributed throughout the world. Brazil, Madagascar and Spain were among their final destinations, the last survivors being in use on a Spanish industrial line until the early 1960s.

The RhB retained two of the 2-8-0s, nos.107 and 108, for engineering and emergency duties. The remainder were sold to Spain, Brazil and Thailand, the latter purchasing eighteen locomotives. Although officially retained as "works" locomotives, the two survivors based at Landquart have for many years been in constant demand for hauling special charter trains on most of the RhB system. They are prohibited, due to the steep gradients, from traversing the Bernina and Arosa lines, otherwise they are likely to appear anywhere between Disentis, St.Moritz, Schuls-Tarasp, Davos and Chur. They quite often work double headed, which is a sight to behold in the dramatic scenery through which they operate. Since 1989, 2-6-0T no.1 has also been available for use on lighter duties or as pilot locomotive for one of the 2-8-0s.

The vintage electric locomotives still in service, notably the "Crocodiles", are equally in demand for hauling historic rolling stock on charter trains. Until quite recently the latter were also utilised on mixed train duties which involved much shunting of freight wagons at each station, in the time honoured tradition.

The fact that historic steam and electric locomotives can successfully work alongside modern machinery, on a railway that incorporates the latest technology in its infrastructure, is a credit to the RhB management. This was demonstrated most clearly in 1989 during the centenary celebrations of the network. The three steam locomotives and some of the vintage electric machines hauled numerous special trains, sharing the intensive timetable with the scheduled service trains. The author's most notable memory of that occasion is of 2-8-0 no.107 being piloted up the 1 in 22 gradient between Klosters and Davos by "Crocodile" no.415. Steam and Electric double heading - it could only happen in Switzerland!

5.1. **FO no.4 and RhB 2-6-0T no.11, with one of the 2-8-0s behind, present a splendid sight at Disentis on 29th July 1968. Although the RhB steam locomotives still occasionally run to this joint station, it is many years since a Furka Oberalp steam hauled train has ventured that far east. (J.Wiseman.)**

5.2.   The RhB depot at Landquart in 1967, had a variety of locomotives gathered around the turntable. From left to right are Ge 6/6 "Crocodile" no.408, 2-8-0 no.108, 2-6-0T no.11 and Ge 4/ 6 no.355. Note the electric catenary converging into a central connection above the turntable. (B.Studer coll./Photoglobe)

5.3. *2-6-0T no.11 was at Landquart depot on 15th October 1966. This locomotive was sold to the* **Bernese Oberland Bahn** *in the early 1970s and is currently based at Zweilütschinen for hauling charter trains on the lower section of the BOB. (P. Sutter/BVA)*

5.4. *RhB rotary snowplough no. X 9212 was at Landquart on the same occasion. This is one of variants that had to be propelled by another locomotive, the steam engine purely being used to drive the rotary plough equipment. This fascinating machine is now based at Gletsch on the Furka Mountain Line, following many years in store at the Blonay-Chamby. (P.Sutter/BVA)*

5.5. *RhB 2-8-0 no.107 hauls a special charter train at Untervaz, between Chur and Landquart, on 17th June 1966. This section of the RhB runs parallel to the SBB main line from Chur to Zurich. (P.Sutter/BVA)*

5.6. No. 107 performs a "photo-run past" near Landquart, during a special excursion from Chur to Davos in conjunction with the centenary celebrations of the RhB, on 23rd September 1989. (J.F.Organ)

5.7. On the same occasion, no.107 waits in the loop at Schiers for a service train to pass. Note the large quantity of briquettes stacked on the relatively small tender. (J.F.Organ)

5.8. No.107 has just arrived at Klosters, on the first leg of the centenary special. The journey between Chur and Davos was interspersed with many stops, mainly in order that the regular timetable was not interrupted. (J.F.Organ)

5.9. *Between Klosters and Davos, a pilot locomotive was required for the special train. This resulted in an interesting combination of electric and steam motive power, with Ge 6/6 "Crocodile" no.415 assisting no.107. (J.F.Organ)*

5.10. *The double headed special waits in the loop at Davos-Laret in order to allow a service train, hauled by a Ge 4/4 11 locomotive, to pass en route to Klosters and Chur. (J.F.Organ)*

5.11. *Two Ge 4/6 electric locomotives nos. 354 and 355, date from 1914, and are seen near Schiers between Klosters and Landquart whilst hauling another special train on 6th April 1974. (P. Sutter/BVA)*

5.12. *A splendid scene at Wiesen viaduct, as 2-8-0s nos. 107 and 108 attack the climb between Filisur and Davos, on 28th June 1969. The 210 metre long viaduct, 88 metres above the Landwasser valley, incorporates a footpath attached to the outer parapet. (P. Sutter/BVA)*

5.13. *A mixed train hauled by two Ge 6/6 "Crocodiles", nos. 415 and 408, pass Rhäzüns in the lower reaches of the Albula valley, with a mixed train on 16th June 1973. (P.Sutter/BVA)*

5.14. *Ge 6/6 "Crocodile" no.415 at Tiefencastel, hauls the weekly afternoon mixed train from Thusis to St.Moritz, on 18th February 1988. Each station stop was a rather protracted affair whilst much shunting of stock was performed. (J.F.Organ)*

5.15. *Often referred to as "honorary steam locomotives", the "Crocodiles" certainly present an interesting appearance with their rod drive and large flywheels. No.415 prepares to leave Tiefencastel bound for St.Moritz. (J.F.Organ)*

5.16. *Another "Crocodile" hauls a train of Pullman coaches across the dramatic Landwasser Viaduct. The coaches were originally supplied to the MOB in 1931 and sold to the RhB just prior to W.W.11. (Photoglobe coll.)*

5.17. *2-8-0s nos.107 and 108 are at Filisur alongside Ge 4/4 1 no.608 on 27th May 1967. These steam hauled special trains are a regular event on the RhB. However, they are often privately chartered and consequently not easy to travel on. (D.Trevor Rowe)*

5.18.   *The two locomotives present an impressive sight as they prepare to leave Filisur and ascend the steep gradients through the Albula Spirals between Bergün and Preda. (D.Trevor Rowe)*

5.19.   *During their return from Preda, the 2-8-0s descend the final stretch of 1 in 29 on the approach to Filisur, on 27th May 1967. (D.Trevor Rowe)*

5.20.   2-8-0 no.108 waits at Bergün as Ge 6/6 11 no.705 passes with a St.Moritz to Chur express. The steam hauled train was part of the centenary celebrations and was returning from St.Moritz on 26th September 1989. (J.F.Organ)

5.21.   This is one of the splendidly restored vintage coaches used by the RhB for their special trains. This four wheeled vehicle dates from the opening of the line in 1889. (J.F.Organ)

5.22.   The two Ge 4/6 locomotives, nos. 354 and 355, approach the lower section of the Albula Spirals, during another stage of their special working on 6th April 1974. (P. Sutter/BVA)

←

5.23.   A Ge 4/4 1 locomotive descends the upper section of the Albula Spirals with a train bound for Chur. The train was about to enter the upper portal of a spiral tunnel, the lower end of which is seen in the foreground. (BVA coll.)

5.24. *Ge 6/6 11 no.705 is in a sylvan setting as it ascends the last section of the Albula Spirals with a Glacier Express bound for St. Moritz on 26th September 1989. The entire length of this dramatic stretch of railway can be viewed from a scenic footpath. (Mrs.B.Organ)*

5.25. *Another Ge 6/6 "Crocodile" no.409, is seen with a mixed train at Preda on 27th May 1967. There was still plenty of snow on the mountains at that time of the year. (D.Trevor Rowe)*

5.26.   *2-6-0T no.1 prepares to leave Samedan with a train bound for Zernez on the Engadine line of the RhB. This train was part of the centenary celebrations on 24th September 1989. (J.F.Organ)*

5.27.   *2-8-0 no.108 was being prepared for its duties at Samedan depot on the same date. The locomotive had worked "light engine" from Landquart during the previous evening. (J.F.Organ).*

5.28.   No.1 and no.108 prepare to double head the last special train of the day from Zernez to Samedan on the same occasion. Due to the intensive programme of specials, fitted between the normal service trains, the timetable had begun to run late. Consequently the last two trains were combined in order to avoid further delays. (J.F.Organ)

5.29.   Briquettes are loaded onto no.108's tender before the two locomotives couple on to the coaches seen in the background during the evening of 24th September 1989. (J.F.Organ)

5.30.   With gradients of 1 in 14, steam locomotives have never been allowed to venture onto the tracks of the Bernina line. A Bernina Express from Tirano to Chur climbs round the final hairpin on the approach to Alp Grüm in September 1988. (J.F.Organ)

5.31.   Here is Brusio spiral viaduct, near the Italian border. A heavy mixed train, bound for Tirano, double headed by a Gem 4/4 electro-diesel locomotive no.802 and an electric railcar passes under the upper part of the loop in September 1988. (J.F.Organ)

5.32.   Electo-diesel Gem 4/4 locomotive no. 801 is at Tirano on 25ᵗʰ September 1989. These dual powered machines are normally based on the Bernina line, but in view of their versatility are often used elsewhere on the RhB system. (J.F.Organ)

5.33.   Rotary snowplough no. X 9213, is assisted by one of the Gem 4/4 electro-diesel locomotive, clearing the track near Pontresina, during February 1990. (R.de Wardt)

5.34. *A more detailed view of no. X 9213 shows it at rest in Pontresina station. This is one of the self-propelled variants of the rotary snowploughs, which incorporated a Meyer type locomotive chassis. Two of these were supplied to the* **Bernina Bahn** *in 1912. The other variation supplied to the RhB, without a locomotive chassis, is illustrated in photograph no. 5.4. (R.de Wardt)*

5.35. *Snow clearing was dramatic action on the Bernina line during the late 1930s. Although obscured by the column of snow and steam, one of the rotary ploughs is obviously in use. (K.Taylorson coll.)*

ENCORE

Although steam locomotives operate throughout the summer months on many of the lines covered in this publication, some of their appearances are irregular. The locomotives retained by the major companies are mainly used to haul charter trains, mainly at weekends, for which advance booking is necessary. Many of these are private charters, including wedding trains, which obviously are not available to the general public. In order to experience steam haulage in Switzerland, the major tourist lines offer the best guarantee. The *Brienz-Rothorn-Bahn* and *Dampfbahn Furka-Bergstrecke* operate a daily service between June and October whilst the *CFT Blonay-Chamby* is in operation at weekends between May and October. The sole steam locomotive on the Rochers De Naye line usually works on a daily basis during high summer. The *CF du Jura* operates a regular timetable of steam hauled excursions during the summer months for which advance booking is recommended.

Ffestiniog Travel, Harbour Station, Porthmadog, LL49 9NF (Tel:-01766 512400) organise escorted holidays to Switzerland three or four times every year. With the excellent rail service available in the country, and with the convenience of a Swiss Travel Pass, it is quite easy to visit many of the railways mentioned in this publication. Anyone wishing to plan their own itinerary, Ffestiniog Travel's Continental Booking Office (Tel:- 01766 516050) can supply tickets and passes to suit. Unfortunately, this does not include tickets for the tourist railways, which have to be purchased locally.

Details of the major tourist and museum railways can be obtained from the following:-

CFT Blonay-Chamby, Case Postale 366, CH 1001 Lausanne, Switzerland. Tel:-(0041) 21 9432121

Brienz-Rothorn-Bahn. Brienz, Switzerland. Tel:- (0041) 33 9522222

Furka-Bergstrecke. DFB, CH-3999 Oberwald / Wallis, Switzerland. Tel:- (0041) 848 000 144

CF du Jura, Case Postale 357, CH-2350 Saignelégier, Switzerland. Tel:- (0041) 32 9524290

Montreux-Rochers De Naye, MOB Montreux, Switzerland. Tel:- (0041) 21 9898181

FURTHER READING

Although there are many publications in German and French relating to the narrow gauge railways of Switzerland, there is surprisingly little currently available in English. Hopefully this book will help to address the situation. Recommended are the following publications.

MOUNTAIN RACK RAILWAYS OF SWITZERLAND	J.R. Bardsley Oakwood Press
CLOUDS ON THE BRIENZER ROTHORN	P.R. Arnold Plateway Press
SWISS MOUNTAIN RAILWAYS	P.J.Kelly Trackside
(Around Luzern and Interlaken).	and D.Binns Publications
MOUNTAIN RAILWAYS AND LOCOMOTIVES	
From Old Picture Postcards	K.Taylorson Plateway Press

BY THE SAME AUTHOR
VIVARAIS NARROW GAUGE
SOUTHERN FRANCE NARROW GAUGE
NORTHERN FRANCE NARROW GAUGE

MP Middleton Press

Easebourne Lane, Midhurst, W Sussex. GU29 9AZ Tel: 01730 813169 Fax: 01730 812601
Email: enquiries@middletonpress.fsnet.co.uk *If books are not available from your
local transport stockist, order direct with cheque, Visa or Mastercard, post free UK.*

BRANCH LINES
Branch Line to Allhallows
Branch Line to Alton
Branch Lines around Ascot
Branch Line to Ashburton
Branch Lines around Bodmin
Branch Line to Bude
Branch Lines around Canterbury
Branch Lines around Chard & Yeovil
Branch Line to Cheddar
Branch Lines around Cromer
Branch Lines to East Grinstead
Branch Lines of East London
Branch Lines to Effingham Junction
Branch Lines around Exmouth
Branch Lines to Falmouth, Helston & St. Ives
Branch Line to Fairford
Branch Lines around Gosport
Branch Line to Hayling
Branch Lines to Henley, Windsor & Marlow
Branch Line to Hawkhurst
Branch Lines around Huntingdon
Branch Line to Ilfracombe
Branch Line to Kingsbridge
Branch Line to Kingswear
Branch Line to Lambourn
Branch Lines to Launceston & Princetown
Branch Lines to Longmoor
Branch Line to Looe
Branch Line to Lyme Regis
Branch Lines around Midhurst
Branch Line to Minehead
Branch Line to Moretonhampstead
Branch Lines to Newport (IOW)
Branch Lines to Newquay
Branch Lines around North Woolwich
Branch Line to Padstow
Branch Lines around Plymouth
Branch Lines to Seaton and Sidmouth
Branch Lines around Sheerness
Branch Line to Shrewsbury
Branch Line to Swanage *updated*
Branch Line to Tenterden
Branch Lines around Tiverton
Branch Line to Torrington
Branch Line to Upwell
Branch Lines of West London
Branch Lines around Weymouth
Branch Lines around Wimborne
Branch Lines around Wisbech

NARROW GAUGE
Branch Line to Lynton
Branch Lines around Portmadoc 1923-46
Branch Lines around Porthmadog 1954-94
Branch Line to Southwold
Douglas to Port Erin
Douglas to Peel
Kent Narrow Gauge
Northern France Narrow Gauge
Romneyrail
Southern France Narrow Gauge
Sussex Narrow Gauge
Surrey Narrow Gauge
Swiss Narrow Gauge
Two-Foot Gauge Survivors
Vivarais Narrow Gauge

SOUTH COAST RAILWAYS
Ashford to Dover

Bournemouth to Weymouth
Brighton to Worthing
Eastbourne to Hastings
Hastings to Ashford
Portsmouth to Southampton
Ryde to Ventnor
Southampton to Bournemouth

SOUTHERN MAIN LINES
Basingstoke to Salisbury
Bromley South to Rochester
Crawley to Littlehampton
Dartford to Sittingbourne
East Croydon to Three Bridges
Epsom to Horsham
Exeter to Barnstaple
Exeter to Tavistock
Faversham to Dover
London Bridge to East Croydon
Orpington to Tonbridge
Tonbridge to Hastings
Salisbury to Yeovil
Sittingbourne to Ramsgate
Swanley to Ashford
Tavistock to Plymouth
Three Bridges to Brighton
Victoria to Bromley South
Victoria to East Croydon
Waterloo to Windsor
Waterloo to Woking
Woking to Portsmouth
Woking to Southampton
Yeovil to Exeter

EASTERN MAIN LINES
Barking to Southend
Ely to Kings Lynn
Ely to Norwich
Fenchurch Street to Barking
Ilford to Shenfield
Ipswich to Saxmundham
Liverpool Street to Ilford
Saxmundham to Yarmouth
Tilbury Loop

WESTERN MAIN LINES
Didcot to Banbury
Didcot to Swindon
Ealing to Slough
Exeter to Newton Abbot
Newton Abbot to Plymouth
Newbury to Westbury
Paddington to Ealing
Paddington to Princes Risborough
Plymouth to St. Austell
Princes Risborough to Banbury
Reading to Didcot
Slough to Newbury
St. Austell to Penzance
Swindon to Bristol
Taunton to Exeter
Westbury to Taunton

MIDLAND MAIN LINES
Euston to Harrow & Wealdstone
St. Pancras to St. Albans

COUNTRY RAILWAY ROUTES
Abergavenny to Merthyr
Andover to Southampton
Bath to Evercreech Junction
Bath Green Park to Bristol
Burnham to Evercreech Junction
Cheltenham to Andover
Croydon to East Grinstead
Didcot to Winchester
East Kent Light Railway
Fareham to Salisbury
Guildford to Redhill
Reading to Basingstoke
Reading to Guildford
Redhill to Ashford
Salisbury to Westbury
Stratford upon Avon to Cheltenham
Strood to Paddock Wood
Taunton to Barnstaple
Wenford Bridge to Fowey
Westbury to Bath
Woking to Alton
Yeovil to Dorchester

GREAT RAILWAY ERAS
Ashford from Steam to Eurostar
Clapham Junction 50 years of change
Festiniog in the Fifties
Festiniog in the Sixties
Festiniog 50 years of enterprise
Isle of Wight Lines 50 years of change
Railways to Victory 1944-46
Return to Blaenau 1970-82
SECR Centenary album
Talyllyn 50 years of change
Yeovil 50 years of change

LONDON SUBURBAN RAILWAYS
Caterham and Tattenham Corner
Charing Cross to Dartford
Clapham Jn. to Beckenham Jn.
Crystal Palace (HL) & Catford Loop
East London Line
Finsbury Park to Alexandra Palace
Holbourn Viaduct to Lewisham
Kingston and Hounslow Loops
Lewisham to Dartford
Lines around Wimbledon
Liverpool Street to Chingford
London Bridge to Addiscombe
Mitcham Junction Lines
North London Line
South London Line
West Croydon to Epsom
West London Line
Willesden Junction to Richmond
Wimbledon to Beckenham
Wimbledon to Epsom

STEAMING THROUGH
Steaming through Cornwall
Steaming through the Isle of Wight
Steaming through Kent
Steaming through West Hants

TRAMWAY CLASSICS
Aldgate & Stepney Tramways
Barnet & Finchley Tramways
Bath Tramways
Brighton's Tramways
Bristol's Tramways
Burton & Ashby Tramways
Camberwell & W.Norwood Tramways
Clapham & Streatham Tramways
Croydon's Tramways
Dover's Tramways
East Ham & West Ham Tramways
Edgware and Willesden Tramways
Eltham & Woolwich Tramways
Embankment & Waterloo Tramways
Enfield & Wood Green Tramways
Exeter & Taunton Tramways
Greenwich & Dartford Tramways
Hammersmith & Hounslow Tramways
Hampstead & Highgate Tramways
Hastings Tramways
Holborn & Finsbury Tramways
Ilford & Barking Tramways
Kingston & Wimbledon Tramways
Lewisham & Catford Tramways
Liverpool Tramways 1. Eastern Routes
Liverpool Tramways 2. Southern Routes
Liverpool Tramways 3. Northern Routes
Maidstone & Chatham Tramways
Margate to Ramsgate
North Kent Tramways
Norwich Tramways
Reading Tramways
Seaton & Eastbourne Tramways
Shepherds Bush & Uxbridge Tramways
Southend-on-sea Tramways
Southwark & Deptford Tramways
Stamford Hill Tramways
Twickenham & Kingston Tramways
Victoria & Lambeth Tramways
Waltham Cross & Edmonton Tramways
Walthamstow & Leyton Tramways
Wandsworth & Battersea Tramways

TROLLEYBUS CLASSICS
Croydon Trolleybuses
Derby Trolleybuses
Hastings Trolleybuses
Huddersfield Trolleybuses
Maidstone Trolleybuses
Portsmouth Trolleybuses
Woolwich & Dartford Trolleybuses

WATERWAY ALBUMS
Kent and East Sussex Waterways
London to Portsmouth Waterway
West Sussex Waterways

MILITARY BOOKS
Battle over Portsmouth
Battle over Sussex 1940
Bombers over Sussex 1943-45
Bognor at War
Military Defence of West Sussex
Military Signals from the South Coast
Secret Sussex Resistance
Surrey Home Guard

OTHER RAILWAY BOOKS
Index to all Middleton Press stations
Industrial Railways of the South-East
South Eastern & Chatham Railways
London Chatham & Dover Railway
London Termini - Past and Proposed
War on the Line (SR 1939-45)

BIOGRAPHY
Garraway Father & Son